SECRETS OF
DISNEYLAND

SECRETS OF DISNEYLAND

WEIRD and
WONDERFUL FACTS
about the
HAPPIEST
PLACE on **EARTH**

DINAH WILLIAMS

STERLING CHILDREN'S BOOKS
New York

STERLING CHILDREN'S BOOKS
New York

An Imprint of Sterling Publishing
387 Park Avenue South
New York, NY 10016

© 2013 by Sterling Publishing Co., Inc.
Original illustration by Eliz Ong
Stock images © Eliz Ong/iStockphoto.com
Design by Rae Ann Spitzenberger

Secrets of Disneyland is an independent publication and is not associated in any way with the Disneyland® Resort, the Disney Company, or any of its affiliates or subsidiaries.

The publisher has made every effort to ensure that the content of this book was current at the time of publication. It is always best to confirm information before making final travel plans as information is always subject to change. The publisher cannot accept responsibility for any consequences arising from the use of this book.

ISBN 978-1-4549-0813-5

Distributed in Canada by Sterling Publishing
c/o Canadian Manda Group, 165 Dufferin Street
Toronto, Ontario, Canada M6K 3H6
Distributed in the United Kingdom by GMC Distribution Services
Castle Place, 166 High Street, Lewes, East Sussex, England BN7 1XU
Distributed in Australia by Capricorn Link (Australia) Pty. Ltd.
P.O. Box 704, Windsor, NSW 2756, Australia

For information about custom editions, special sales, and premium and corporate purchases, please contact Sterling Special Sales at 800-805-5489 or specialsales@sterlingpublishing.com.

Manufactured in China
Lot #:
2 4 6 8 10 9 7 5 3 1
08/13

www.sterlingpublishing.com/kids

CONTENTS

> "Disneyland is dedicated to the ideals, the dreams, and the hard facts that have created America, with the hope that it will be a source of joy and inspiration to all the world."
>
> **—WALT DISNEY**

INTRODUCTION

Disneyland opened in Anaheim, California, in 1955. Since its opening, Walt Disney and his team of Imagineers have worked nonstop to make your visit a happy one. Disney believed in the idea of "plussing," or making an idea better. Everywhere you look at Disneyland, you can see plussing in action. Disney Imagineers

are always working to improve the rides and attractions. They want to make the park the most magical place for families to visit time and time again.

In *Secrets of Disneyland*, we've uncovered tons of behind-the-scenes tidbits and fascinating facts that make the park special. We hope you'll enjoy learning the secrets behind "the Happiest Place on Earth"!

DISNEY·LAND PARK

Walt Disney's original idea was to build an **8-acre** Mickey Mouse Park near the Disney Studios.

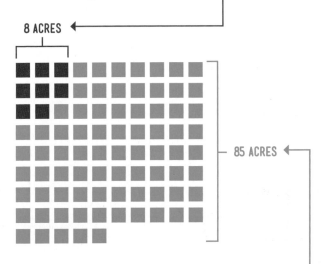

8 ACRES

85 ACRES

But the more he dreamed, the bigger it grew. Disneyland opened on **85 acres** on July 17, 1955.

Disneyland was built in just **365 days**. On opening day, people started to line up at 2 AM. Dave MacPherson, the park's first visitor, received a **lifetime pass**. Since then, more than **500 million** people have visited "the Happiest Place on Earth."

Disneyland opened with **5** lands and **18** major attractions. Today, there are **8** lands and more than **60** adventures and attractions. Fourteen of the original **18** attractions are **still open**.

Many U.S. presidents have visited Disneyland. These include **Harry S. Truman**, **Dwight D. Eisenhower**, **John F. Kennedy**, **Richard Nixon**, **Jimmy Carter**, **Ronald Reagan**, and **George H. W. Bush**. All 43 presidents are currently performing at the **Hall of Presidents**!

When Disneyland was being built, Walt Disney had an **apartment** created for his family. It was built over the fire station on Main Street, U.S.A. When Disney was there, he would leave **a light burning** in the window. Since his death in 1966, the light has been left on **in his memory**.

A **fireman's pole** connected Disney's apartment to the **firehouse** below it. The top of the pole was sealed after a **guest climbed up** to meet the Disney family.

The **Disneyland Band**
has been performing an
average of four shows a day
since 1955. During those
90,000 performances,
they've marched **3,500**
miles and played **400**
different songs.

Quick QUIZ

Every employee that works at Disneyland is called a cast member. No matter the job, every cast member wears a name tag. This includes the horses that pull the trolleys down Main Street, U.S.A. and the goats of Big Thunder Ranch. Can you guess how many people work at Disneyland?

a) 15,000   **b)** 10,000

c) 20,000   **d)** 18,000

Answer: c

If you ask cast members **a question** about Disney or the theme park, they **must give you an answer**. They are not allowed to say "I don't know." There are cast member phones they can use to call Disneyland **operators for help** with their response.

In 1963, Disneyland's **Enchanted Tiki Room** was the first attraction to use **Audio-Animatronic** figures. This is a type of robot developed by Disney. The **birds** in the Tiki Room can move their beaks and eyes.

Disneyland **wardrobe** has approximately **800,000** costumes. This includes outfits for the **650** Audio-Animatronic figures. The wardrobe people are very busy. Nearly **150,000** pieces and **300,000** buttons have to be replaced each year!

More than **3,000** Disneyland cast members **can speak a language** other than English. Their second language is listed on their name tag. **More than 30 different languages** are spoken at Disneyland. These include Russian, Korean, Portuguese, and even Zulu.

The design and creative team for Disney are called **Imagineers**. They build all rides, resorts, and parks. The word is a combination of **"imagination"** and **"engineer."**

Disneyland's **Lost and Found** collects about **200,000 items** a year. The most common things are hats and sunglasses. They also find up to **300 cell phones** a week! The weirdest finds include a glass eyeball, **$3,000 in cash**, a waterbed, and a toilet seat! Disneyland **donates unclaimed items** to Goodwill charities.

Millions of pairs of **Mickey Mouse ears** have been sold at Disneyland. There have been **200 different styles**, including one introduced in 2012 called "Glow with the Show." The ears on this hat **change color** to match the shows at Disneyland.

The first **Hidden Mickeys began as jokes** among Walt Disney Imagineers. They would **hide pictures** of Mickey Mouse when they were designing an attraction. Word spread and now you can spend your entire trip **hunting for Mickey**!

Are you **celebrating your birthday** at Disneyland? Visit City Hall on your way in. They'll give you a **special birthday pin**. If you wear it, expect birthday greetings from cast members! You can also have a **birthday party** at Disneyland Park's Plaza Inn. Mickey and Minnie Mouse could be two of your guests!

Gum has **never been sold** at Disneyland. Walt didn't want people to get **gum stuck** on their shoes. He also didn't want his **cleaning crews** to have to spend time scraping it up.

How many brooms does the cleaning crew use each year to keep Disneyland clean? **More than 1,000.** They also use about 500 dustpans and 3,000 mops. Every day, they pick up 30 tons of trash. Every night, they steam clean all of the streets.

Nearly **200 wild cats** live at Disneyland and California Adventure Park. They are **fed at five stations** throughout the parks. The cats are allowed to stay because they **control the mice population**. Don't tell Mickey Mouse!

Pin trading can be a lot of fun. First, buy a Disney pin. Then find a cast member with a lanyard who has a pin you want. You can trade your pin for the cast member's. According to the rules, you may trade up to two pins with each cast member. Only kids ages 3–12 can trade with the cast members wearing green lanyards.

Each year Disneyland serves an incredible amount of food and drink, including:

4 million
burgers

★ ★ ★

3 million
orders of fries

★ ★ ★

1 million
gallons of soda

★ ★ ★

1.6 million
hot dogs

★ ★ ★

2.8 million
churros

3.2 million
servings of ice cream

Want to get married at Disneyland?
You can! The bakery makes nearly
250 wedding cakes a year.

MAIN ST.

MAIN STREET, U.S.A.

Main Street, U.S.A. was based on **Walt Disney's hometown** of Marceline, Missouri. The Main Street Opera House is the **oldest building** in Disneyland. It was originally the park's lumber mill from **1955 to 1961**.

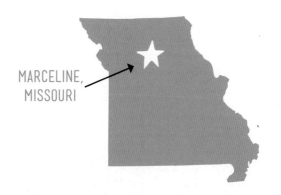

MARCELINE, MISSOURI

FIREWORKS
Facts

There are currently **six different fireworks shows** at Disneyland:

✔ **"Remember. . . Dreams Come True"** (winter and spring)

✔ **"Magical"** (summer)

✔ **"Disney's Celebrate America!"** (Fourth of July)

✔ **"Halloween Screams"** (fall)

✔ **"Believe . . . in Holiday Magic"** (December)

✔ **"Ring in the New Year"** (New Year's Eve)

On Main Street, U.S.A., you can't miss the **delicious smells** coming from the Candy Palace and Gibson Girl Ice Cream Parlor. While **some smells are natural**, others are pumped out into the street through vents. The **vanilla scent** is used most of the year. During the holiday season, a **peppermint scent** fills the air.

In a **light fixture** in the Market House, see if you can find the Hidden Mickeys in the middle.

★ ★ ★

Check out the **jeweled lamp** in the Gibson Girl Ice Cream Parlor. The jewels form many Hidden Mickeys.

In the Silhouette Studio, there is a **leather picture frame**. Inside, three circles form a Mickey head.

★ ★ ★

Look underneath the **fruit cart** on Main Street. There's a Hidden Mickey between the **wheels**.

Did you know that Disneyland used to have **its own postmark**? When you mailed a postcard on Main Street, it received a **Disneyland stamp**. There also used to be a printing press that published a **newspaper**. It was called *The Disneyland News* and was published monthly from 1955 to 1957.

The **five steam-powered trains** on the Disneyland Railroad are the C.K. Holliday, E. P. Ripley, Ernest S. Marsh, Fred Gurley, and Ward Kimball. The **caboose** at the end of the C.K. Holliday train is a **fancy car**. It is named the Lilly Belle, after Walt's wife Lillian.

Quick QUIZ

The bench in the Opera House used to be located in Los Angeles. It was next to the merry-go-round in Griffith Park. While sitting on it, Walt Disney_____.

a) saw a mouse and named it Mickey

b) came up with the idea for Disneyland

c) met a woman who looked like Snow White

d) decided to make Space Mountain in the dark

Answer: b

How many people are in Mickey's Soundsational Parade? **More than 100**, including dancers, drummers, musicians, puppeteers, and Disney characters. This **23-minute musical parade** travels between "it's a small world" and Town Square. The opening drumline is followed by nine floats that celebrate Disney songs.

Each year at the holidays,
Disneyland is especially festive. This
is accomplished with the help of:

79,000
ornaments decorating
Main Street

* * *

2,365
ornaments on the
Christmas tree

* * *

2,015 feet
of garland

* * *

7,410 feet
(nearly 1½ miles)
of ribbon used
for **812** bows

10,395
lights

★ ★ ★

10 cast members
who do nothing
but create holiday
decorations all
year long

FANTASY
LAND

When **Walt Disney** opened Fantasyland in 1955, it was **broadcasted on TV**. He said:

> " Fantasyland is dedicated to the young and the young at heart, and to those who believe that when you wish upon a star, your dreams do come true. "

The **drawbridge** on Sleeping Beauty Castle is real. It has been **raised and lowered** only twice. The first time was when the park first opened in **1955**. The second time was in **1983** when Fantasyland was fixed up and reopened.

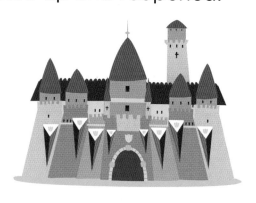

Word Search

Find the names of some of the boats from Storybook Land Canal Boats in the word search.

```
W H L Q E O A S L J Y Z V A Z
K I F L G M J O F W H S K P P
I W J D T A B W J X Q S E U H
B L E A R I E L P Y S X R E G
X L E L L E B P F U R E H F V
R A U Y Z K X A V V W U M J V
F B H E A V A I U O T F N O C
H O O C V I Y Z L R A X Z M G
Y V M I E W H F N U O R L L R
E O Y L S F S K N E C R O W O
P N M A L J S A S U O Z A O K
O Q I O U I E W D N J I X Y B
U C R L W D F G O S S C Z R I
B A Z K A M E M T Y E F M H B
L O Y M B F C G W Z H H L P Q
```

Alice   Faline

Ariel   Fauna

Aurora   Flora

Belle   Flower

Check the answer key on page 158
to see the completed word search.

There are **18 teacups** on the Mad Tea Party ride. You control the speed, but the **orange diamond** and **lavender cups** spin the fastest. The ride is not covered, so it closes when it rains.

Casey Jr. Circus Train has been chugging around the outside of Storybook Land since **1955**. The ride is based on a train from the 1941 film *Dumbo*. Some of the cars were taken from King Arthur Carrousel. As it climbs the hills, it says, **"I think I can!"** just like *The Little Engine That Could*.

Quick QUIZ

The 68 horses on King Arthur Carrousel were hand-carved in 1922. Each of them is repainted every two years. How long does it take to paint each one?

a) 20 hours

b) 30 hours

c) 40 hours

d) 50 hours

The **lead horse** on King Arthur Carrousel is named **Jingles**. You can spot her by the string of bells she wears. She was **painted gold** for Disneyland's 50th anniversary.

Sword in the Stone
is located outside of King
Arthur Carrousel. Merlin
the Magician challenges
everyone to **pull out the
sword**. If you do, you
are named the **"Ruler
of the Realm."** No,
you do not get to rule
Disneyland! However, you
do get a special medal
and certificate.

During **Snow White's Scary Adventures**, the evil queen is seen more often than Snow White! Snow White appears only in the beginning of the ride. This is because guests are seeing the action from **Snow White's point of view**. If you touch the apple on the bookstand, you'll hear the sound of thunder and the laugh of the **evil queen**.

What was one of the most stolen props in Fantasyland? The evil queen's **poisoned apple** in Snow White's Scary Adventures. It has been taken so many times that it was **replaced with a hologram** of an apple.

When Pinocchio **wished upon a star**, his dream came true. In **Pinocchio's Daring Journey**, you visit all of the highlights on his journey to become a real boy. Along the way, you meet **32** animated characters, **29** animated props, and numerous special effects.

On **Alice in Wonderland**, there used to be a **caterpillar** sitting on top of the mushroom. This is where the book *A Very Merry Unbirthday to You* is now placed. The caterpillar was relocated but **his foot was forgotten**! Look closely and you will see that it's still on the mushroom.

Guests love **Dumbo the Flying Elephant** ride. It is one of the park's original attractions. The 16 elephants are **controlled by the guests**, who decide how high an elephant flies. Originally the elephants' **ears moved**. However, they broke often. In 1963, new Dumbos were made without flapping ears.

Matterhorn Bobsleds was the first rollercoaster in the world to use a **steel, tube-shaped track**. It is also the first rollercoaster to have a **basketball court** inside! The basketball court was built inside of the mountain for cast members to use on their breaks. It was removed in 2000 when Matterhorn Bobsleds needed repairs.

Quick QUIZ

The Matterhorn is 147 feet tall. The original mountain in the Swiss Alps is 14,700 feet tall. More than 800 gallons of paint were recently added to give the mountain more "snow." What material was added to the paint to give it some sparkle?

a) glass beads

b) aluminum foil

c) small mirrors

d) chips of ice

Answer: a

The **"it's a small world"** boat ride takes guests through **seven continents**. More than 300 dolls in native dress sing the song "It's a Small World (After All)." Each doll sings in its **country's language**. The ride was originally designed for the 1964/1965 **World's Fair** in New York. It opened in Disneyland in 1966. The same ride opened at Walt Disney World in Florida in 1971.

When "it's a small world" was updated in 2008, 30 Disney characters were added in their native lands. Ariel is now found under water. Pinocchio is in Italy. Cinderella is in France. And England hosts Alice, the White Rabbit, Peter Pan, and Tinker Bell.

"it's a small world"
HOLIDAY

Each year, "it's a small world" is decorated for the holiday season.

- ✓ **50,000** lights are used on the outside of the building.

- ✓ There are **250,000** to **500,000** lights used on the inside.

- ✓ It takes **12** cast members up to **8** weeks to decorate the ride.

- ✓ **75,000** lights are used for the snowflake tree.

Sleeping Beauty Castle is only 77 feet tall. However, it looks larger because of a **building trick**. The higher up you look on the castle, the smaller the windows or bricks get. This makes the castle **look even taller** when you look at it from the ground.

In the line for Mr. Toad's
Wild Ride, look into
**Mr. Toad's left
eye** to see a red
Hidden Mickey.

★ ★ ★

As you fly over Big
Ben on Peter Pan's
Flight, you will see
Mickey's **shadow
in a window** near
the top.

In Pinocchio's
Daring Journey, three
pieces of popcorn
in the machine form
an **upside-down**
Mickey head.

★ ★ ★

When the roses are
painted red in Alice
in Wonderland,
the **splatters** form
a Hidden Mickey.

Quick QUIZ

Storybook Land Canal Boats takes you past famous places from Disney movies. All of the boats are named after Disney characters. They are all girls, except for one. Can you guess which boat is the only one named after a male character? The answer may surprise you!

a) Flora

b) Aurora

c) Belle

d) Flower

Answer: d

Tiny Kline was the first Tinker Bell to fly from the top of the Matterhorn at the beginning of the "Fantasy in the Sky" fireworks show in 1961. At the time, she was 70 years old! The 4′ 10″ woman was a former circus performer. She retired in 1964.

Since the closing of the Skyway, there is only one attraction at Disneyland on which you **hang from above**: Peter Pan's Flight. The **pirate ships** swing from an overhead rail. You feel **like you are flying** over London and Never Land.

For the **40th** anniversary of Disneyland in 1995, a special **time capsule** was created. Shaped like Sleeping Beauty Castle, the capsule contained many items from Disneyland. It was **buried in the courtyard** of the castle. It will be opened on the 80th anniversary of Disneyland on **July 17, 2035**.

TOMORROW
LAND

When Disneyland opened in **1955**, Tomorrowland represented what the **future in 1986** would be like. However, its construction was rushed. Tomorrowland did not turn out as Imagineers had hoped. In 1967, they **rebuilt the entire area** and created a whole new Tomorrowland.

Autopia is the only original Tomorrowland attraction. This ride allows guests to drive on the highways of the future. The attraction that opened for the shortest period of time was the Viewliner. The Viewliner was a fast miniature train. It only lasted one year.

Quick QUIZ

The 124 different cars at Autopia reach a maximum speed of 7 miles per hour on a 4-lane track. You drive along Route 55, which is a tribute to _____.

a) the year Disneyland opened, 1955

b) how many people an hour can go on the ride

c) the number of seconds it takes to make one lap around the track

d) how old Walt Disney was when he created Mickey Mouse

Answer: a

The **speakers** on
the Space Mountain
cars form
Mickey heads.

★ ★ ★

In the Buzz Lightyear
Astro Blasters line, the
planet Skadenii has
a continent in the shape
of a Hidden Mickey.

★ ★ ★

While watching the
demonstration on new
computers at Innoventions,
look for **three gears** on
the wall in the shape
of a Mickey head.

At Innoventions, check
out the **shoelaces** on
Tom Morrow. See if you
can spot the **pattern**
of Mickey heads.

The **rocket-spinner**
attraction has been called
Astro Jets, Rocket Jets,
and Tomorrowland Jets.
It was finally named
Astro Orbitor in 1998.
The design was based
on drawings by the artist
Leonardo da Vinci.

The Innoventions **rotating theater** moves at a speed of **1 mile per hour**. The outside of the bottom floor makes a full revolution every **17** minutes and **40** seconds.

Word Search

Disneyland has a fleet of eight submarines. Find all the names of the submarines in the word search.

```
H E O C P V F R N N H W X H L
H K U F N E E D K A I X V A S
I F F I E R Q I E U M N J E E
V S L P O X V Q R T U E M J R
Q G E L L B X E N I S C O U T
N V P Q D L R Z X L R D D Y L
N X E K M A F W H U A M X Z V
E P Y S F H T L E S F H Y B P
S N C A J V V U R A H B H J J
Q C E I R O Q E A Z M X Z A O
O S Q I Y W N F F N H D G T U
M Y Y A W I R K M K O R K T M
L Q G P R H W B T D A G V U Y
U E Y A N E P T U N E F R O P
R W M Z Z H J Z V P Y A L A N
```

Argonaut   Neptune
Explorer   Scout
Mariner   Seafarer
Nautilus   Voyager

Check the answer key on page 158 to see the completed word search.

How much do you know about **Star Wars**? Audio-Animatronic C-3PO at Star Tours used to have two gold legs. However, Star Wars fans let cast members know that it wasn't correct. So one of **C-3PO's legs** is now silver instead. Cool fact: The **R2-D2** droid who accompanies him is the same one that appeared in the Star Wars movies.

The lagoon for **Finding Nemo** Submarine Voyage holds about **6.3 million gallons** of water. Imagineers created a special paint made with recycled glass for the rocks and coral in the water.

Space Mountain is a 118-foot-high rollercoaster that races through the **darkness of space**. The ride opened in 1977 and was made even faster in 2005. **Neil Armstrong**, the first man to walk on the moon, was a special guest at the reopening!

The Disneyland Monorail is a great way to see the park from above. Here are some fun facts about these high-tech trains:

The Monorail carries **110,000** passengers on an average day.

★ ★ ★

Each train holds up to **132** people.

★ ★ ★

The round trip is **2.5** miles and takes **13** minutes. It has a **99.9** percent "on time" rate.

The trains reach
an average of
30 miles per hour.

★ ★ ★

The Monorail system
turned **50** in 2009.

When opening Tomorrowland, **Walt Disney** imagined the future would be short on space for **growing food**. If you look closely at the plants in Tomorrowland, you'll find that you can eat most of them. There are **strawberries**, lemons, oranges, **pineapple**, guava, papaya, peppers, and **kale**, among others.

Star Tours has 50 different possible ride **combinations** through places and events in the Star Wars movies. You can ride it **again and again** and not get the same ride twice. When in line for Star Tours, you may hear an announcer call for "Mr. Egroeg Sacul." That's movie director **George Lucas** spelled backward!

NEW ORLEANS SQUARE

Keep an ear out in New Orleans Square for all of the performers, including the **Jambalaya Jazz Band**. Want to hear the songs from *The Princess and the Frog*, which took place in New Orleans? **Princess Tiana's Mardi Gras Celebration** makes its way through the Square.

There is an **exclusive club** called Club 33 above the **Blue Bayou** restaurant in New Orleans Square. The membership costs thousands of dollars. People have to wait for many years just to get on the **waiting list**! Club 33 members and their guests get free entrance to Disneyland and other perks.

Quick QUIZ

The cast members at the Haunted Mansion are the only employees at Disneyland encouraged not to smile. How many ghosts are said to live in the haunted house?

a) 666   **b)** 100

c) 999   **d)** 800

Answer: c

Want to see a pet cemetery? Look to the right of the Haunted Mansion and you find tombstones that read:

✔ "Freddie the Bat,
   We'll Miss You, 1847"

✔ "Old Flybait, He Croaked,
   August 9, 1869"

✔ "Here lies my snake whose fatal mistake was frightening the gardener who carried a rake"

✔ "Here lies long-legged Jeb, got tangled up in his very own web"

The **voice** and the face of the **fallen bust** in the Haunted Mansion is not Walt Disney, as many believe. It is **Thurl Ravenscroft**, who sang the Christmas classic "You're a Mean One, Mr. Grinch" from *How the Grinch Stole Christmas!* His was also the voice of **Tony the Tiger** for Frosted Flakes cereal.

Do you know how the spirits in the ballroom were made to dance? It is an old magician's trick called **Pepper's Ghost**. The Audio-Animatronics are dancing in the space above and below the ballroom. They are lit so their **images are reflected** in a 30-foot-tall pane of glass in front of you.

Some of the Haunted Mansion is actually located **outside of Disneyland**. As you walk through the portrait hall, you're really walking **under Disney's railroad tracks**. The hall leads to a building outside the park.

The **plates on the ballroom table** in the Haunted Mansion form the shape of Mickey's head.

★ ★ ★

In the first room of the Haunted Mansion, look for the **candlestick holders** on the wall. View one from below and you'll see a Hidden Mickey.

In the last room of
Pirates of the Caribbean, there
is **armor** hanging on the
wall. The **gold one** has
a Mickey in the design
on the chest.

★ ★ ★

When the Haunted
Mansion changes for
the Christmas holidays,
there is a **stained glass
picture of a tree** added
to the stretching room. The
red ornaments form
a Hidden Mickey.

Did you notice the **ship's anchor** in New Orleans Square? A sign says it is from **Jean Lafitte's pirate ship**, taken during the Battle of New Orleans in 1815. The sign also states, "Don't believe everything you read"!

Building **New Orleans Square**, including Pirates of the Caribbean, cost **$18 million**. That is more than the United States paid for the real New Orleans in the Louisiana Purchase of 1803!

The Pirates of the Caribbean is the last attraction that Walt Disney had a hand in designing before his death. Here are some more facts about this pirate adventure:

This **15-minute** boat ride set in the 1850s can handle **3,400** guests an hour.

There are **53** Audio-
Animatronic animals and
birds and **75** Audio-Animatronic
pirates and villagers.

★ ★ ★

Your boat drops down
a **52-foot** waterfall
and then a second
37-foot drop.

★ ★ ★

Keep an eye out
for **Jack Sparrow**.
He appears at least
three times
during the ride!

During the battles in Pirates of the Caribbean, **cannons splash** into the water around you. However, real cannonballs are not used. The effect is a combination of a **flash of light** with a **blast of air** from under the water.

More than **311 million** guests have ridden the **Pirates of the Caribbean** since it opened in April 1967. Walt Disney had originally planned for it to be a **wax museum**. It became a ride after the popularity of "it's a small world."

ADVENTURE
LAND

The **Enchanted Tiki Room** is one of the original attractions at Disneyland. To run the Audio-Animatronics in 1963, **huge computers** were used. In order to keep the computers cool, the room was the first at Disneyland to be **air-conditioned**.

The **Tiki Juice Bar** is one of the few places in the world that serves a **Dole Whip**. This pineapple soft-serve is so loved that it has its own **fan T-shirt**. The shirt is also sold mainly at Disney parks.

On the **Jungle Cruise**, listen closely while you are **ambushed by natives**. If the jungle is quiet enough, you will hear one of them say **"I love disco!"**

In the show room
of the line for Indiana
Jones, there is a huge
Hidden Mickey on the
wall near the screen.

★ ★ ★

Look for **three
barnacles** under
the letter *J* on the
sign for the Jungle
Cruise that form a
Hidden Mickey.

In Tarzan's Treehouse, in the room where Tarzan is being drawn, is a **chest with a keyhole** in the shape of Mickey's head.

Quick QUIZ

On the Jungle Cruise, keep your eyes open during the Lost Expedition part of the ride. There is a crate behind the gorillas that reads "WED Expedition." What does *WED* stand for?

a) Wild Elephant Doctor

b) Walt Elias Disney

c) West, East, or Down

d) Water's End Direction

Answer: b

One of the many **palm trees** in the jungle at Adventureland is more than **115 years old**. When Disney bought the land from the Dominguez family, there was a date palm that had been planted in **1896**. As part of the deal, Disney agreed not to cut it down. It now towers over Adventureland.

You can follow **Indiana Jones** on his quest for the Jewel of Power. The goddess Mara looks into the souls of visitors and grants one of **three treasures**: gold, eternal youth, or knowledge of the future. Which she chooses for you is the basis for this ever-changing ride. There are nearly **160,000 possible adventures**.

See if you can spot the **Eeyore signs**! Indiana Jones Adventure is built where the Eeyore section of the Disneyland **parking lot** was once located. Three Eeyore signs have been left. Two are in the **movie room** and one is on the **ride**.

The **jeeps** in Indiana Jones Adventure seem to move **backward**. However, the walls are actually moving forward. Want to see how it's done? Turn around and **look backward** while the ride is moving.

The Indiana Jones Adventure is jam-packed with interesting things. There are more than **1,300** props, **2,000** fake skulls, and **2,000** different snakes. One of the most famous props is a **skeleton named Bones** in the mummy chamber. He wears a Mickey Mouse ear hat with his name embroidered on it!

If you'd like a look inside Tarzan's home, check out Tarzan's Treehouse.

The fake tree that holds the house weighs **150 tons** and is about **70 feet tall**. From the top you can see most of Adventureland.

★ ★ ★

The **450 branches** contain **6,000 leaves** that were applied by hand.

The base of the tree is
90 feet wide and the
roots go **42 feet** into
the ground.

★ ★ ★

Tarzan's is one of
four treehouses in
Disneyland. Chip and Dale
have a treehouse, as do Tom
and Huck. There is also the
**Treehouse of
Technology** at Innoventions
in Tomorrowland.

Want to know how to fix what bothers you? Put **50 cents** into the **witch doctor's machine** in Adventureland Bazaar. The **shrunken head** of Dr. Nedley Lostmore will tell you what's wrong and print you a prescription.

Tarzan's Treehouse used to be the **Swiss Family Robinson Treehouse**. In 1999 it was remade when the film *Tarzan* was released. There remains a **gramophone** in the laboratory that plays the **"Swisskapolka."** This song is from the 1960 movie *Swiss Family Robinson*.

CRITTER
COUNTRY

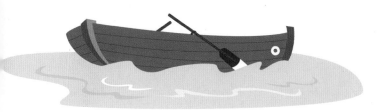

When Critter Country
originally opened in **1956**,
it was called **Indian
Village**. Different
tribes would perform
ceremonial dances. You
could also see real teepees
and totem poles, and
paddle an **Indian war
canoe**. It closed in 1971.

The **Country Bear Jamboree** was closed to make way for The Many Adventures of **Winnie the Pooh**. As a tribute to the Jamboree, they mounted the heads of three of the Jamboree characters at the exit of the Heffalumps and Woozles area. Look up and you will see **Max** (a buck), **Buff** (a buffalo), and **Melvin** (a moose).

The Pooh Corner shop sells treats called **Tigger Tails**. They are one of the most popular snacks in the park. To make them, **marshmallows** are dipped into **caramel** and **white chocolate**. Then they are covered in orange sugar **sprinkles** and dark chocolate **stripes**. They look just like Tigger's tail but taste much better.

Finding
HIDDEN MICKEY

In the entrance tunnel at the beginning of the Winnie the Pooh ride, there is a Hidden Mickey painted in the **tree trunk on your right**.

★ ★ ★

At the end of the Winnie the Pooh ride, there is a Heffalump collage on the right. Look at the **bottom right corner** for **three circles** that make up the head of your favorite mouse.

The **hole** where you come out for the final drop in Splash Mountain is cut in the **shape of Mickey's head**.

★ ★ ★

When you are in line for Splash Mountain and walk into the building, on the left there is a **set of gears** that form a Hidden Mickey.

Word Search

Find your favorite Winnie the Pooh characters in the word search.

```
F Y K A G Z J H J B X M Q X K
O P G D E U S R E H Y Z M W A
Z O A B E Y O M F K Y J M Z N
H O I W I T T P G Z I I A R G
E H J Q D Z Q U B A I S O A A
E L B W Q D S M Y S Q C I B J
Q N D R P I Y Z A I H E S B M
I V R C F H I T E L G I P I F
X E E Y O R E I A D L L V T P
O B U R E G G I T W N K W S A
K Q Z K U A S A O Y Q Q Z V W
Q M F M Y G F Y D D M P A F C
F Z Z A Z M S U J S D H P U O
C G Z Y Q Z A I Z Q F Q S P C
Q Z L A Z Z O K U Q K O O R S
```

Eeyore   Pooh
Kanga   Rabbit
Owl   Roo
Piglet   Tigger

Check the answer key on page 158
to see the completed word search.

Davy Crockett's **35-foot-long canoes** are the only **guest-powered** ride in Disneyland. Every one of the 20 passengers is expected to **paddle**.

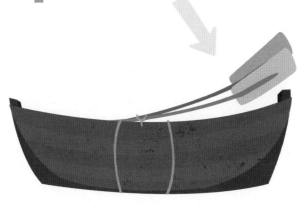

Critter Country's Splash
Mountain delivers plenty of
critters. Guests follow
Brer Rabbit and his animal
friends from the movie
Song of the South.
Here are some more facts
about this musical log
flume adventure:

The ride contains a
five-story drop
that reaches speeds
of **40** miles per hour.

The ride is **87** feet
high and **2,800** feet long.
More than **100**
Audio-Animatronics
fill the attraction.

★ ★ ★

The ride cost
$75 million
to create in 1989.

★ ★ ★

The showboat
in the finale
is **50** feet wide
and **30** feet high.

MICKEY'S TOON-TOWN

There are a lot of fun surprises in Toontown, which opened in 1993.

★ ★ ★

Don't miss the **water fountain** just outside the bathrooms by Goofy's Gas Station.

★ ★ ★

You can also pick up the **police telephone** and listen to people reporting crimes.

Touch away in Toontown! You can press the **plunger** on the **TNT detonator** outside the Fireworks Factory. You can also push the **doorbell** for the Toontown Glass Works and open the **mailbox** at the post office.

Jump into a **giant roller skate** and get ready to roll. Gadget's Go Coaster is **28 feet high** and reaches **22 miles per hour** before the ride has ended.

In the telephone booth, the **center of the dial** has Mickey's head on it.

In Minnie's House,
check out the food
in her **refrigerator**.
There is a bottle of
cheese relish
with Mickey's head
on the front.

★ ★ ★

In Mickey's house,
look at the **player
piano paper**. The
holes are all Hidden
Mickeys!

★ ★ ★

In the first room of
Mickey's house, see if
you can find the **book**
with the Hidden Mickey
on the spine.

The license plates on the wall of Roger Rabbit's Car Toon Spin refer to Disney characters or movies. Can you guess what these license plates are code for?

2N TOWN   _____

BB WOLF   _____

1DRLND   _____

L MERM8   _____

In **Roger Rabbit Car Toon Spin**, you climb in a taxicab named Lenny for a wild ride through the **back alleys** of Toontown. The cars spin clockwise and counterclockwise. But no matter how hard you try, the cars will **never spin** as quickly as the cups on Mad Tea Party.

FRONTIER LAND

When Frontierland opened in **1955**, there was an attraction called **Mule Pack** on which guests rode mules. In 1963 it was made larger and renamed **Pack Mules Through Nature's Wonderland**. The ride closed in **1973**. There is still a sign that reads "Pack Mules—Bought, Sold, & Rented"!

Fantasmic! is an amazing
light and water show
that takes place at night.

Fantasmic! features
50 performers
and **50 backstage
crew members**.

★ ★ ★

Fantasmic lasts
about **22** minutes
and costs **$75,000**
to produce each night.

★ ★ ★

The fire-breathing
dragon is **45 feet long**.

**Thirty-five-
foot-tall**
mist screens are
used as screens
for movies.

★ ★ ★

9,000 people
can watch
the show at
one time.

★ ★ ★

Kaa the snake is
100 feet long.

Quick QUIZ

On Big Thunder Mountain Railroad, the runaway mine car can reach speeds of about 30 miles per hour through the Old West. The wildest ride is in the last of the five cars. Which one of the following is not the name of a train?

I. M. Brave

I. B. Hearty

I. M. Bold

R. U. Chicken

U. R. Fearless

U. R. Daring

Answer: R. U. Chicken

Big Thunder Ranch petting zoo near the BBQ restaurant is home to cows, goats, and pigs. In 2005 it also became home to **two famous turkeys**! When the president pardoned two turkeys on **Thanksgiving** that year, they were the first to go live at Frontierland.

On the stage at the
Golden Horseshoe
Saloon, there is a
grate in the front
that contains a small
Hidden Mickey.

★ ★ ★

The Mark Twain
Riverboat has
two Hidden Mickeys
in the **decorative
ironwork** between
the smokestacks.

★ ★ ★

If you are on the
river, there are **three
round river rocks**
in the water making
a Mickey head.

In Big Thunder
Ranch petting zoo,
there is a Hidden Mickey
in the **wooden
sink counter**.

Doritos were invented in Frontierland! The chip company Frito-Lay opened **Casa de Fritos**, a Mexican restaurant, in Disneyland in 1955. The restaurant fried up **extra tortillas** cut into chips. The snack was such a hit that Frito-Lay began selling them across the country in **1966**.

The **musical** *Golden Horseshoe Revue* played at the **saloon** from 1955 to 1986. It logged **over 50,000 performances** and made it into the *Guinness World Records* for the longest-running live stage show of all time.

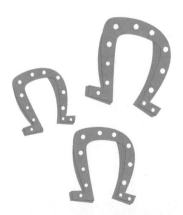

Opened in **2001**, Disney California Adventure Park hoped to capture **everything wonderful** about the state. However, people **did not love** this new park. Some said it lacked magic. In **2007** Disney began a huge redesign, which cost more than **$1.1 billion**. The park was reopened in **2012**.

On Buena Vista Street, catch a ride on the **Red Car Trolley**. These are replicas of the Pacific Electric Railway cars famous in southern California. The numbers on the trolleys refer to **important dates** in Disney history. For example, car **623** refers to the month and year that Walt Disney came to Los Angeles: **June 1923.**

Quick QUIZ

In Ariel's Undersea Adventure, there are 183 Audio-Animatronic figures. Of these, 49 are spinning starfish. Ursula is the largest in the show at 7½ feet tall and 12 feet wide. The cars that carry you through the ride are designed to look like _____.

a) starfish   **b)** clam shells

c) seahorses   **d)** dolphins

Although California Screamin' is built to look like an old wooden rollercoaster, it is actually very high tech.

5.8 million pounds of steel and **11.5 million** pounds of concrete were used to build the rollercoaster.

★ ★ ★

The fastest speed is **55** miles per hour and the biggest drop is **108** feet.

The length of the track
is **6,072** feet, the **8th**
longest in the world.

★ ★ ★

Each year the coaster
travels **50,000** miles.

★ ★ ★

Music pulses out of
108 speakers
on each train.

★ ★ ★

The coaster goes from
zero to **55** miles per hour
in **four** seconds.

Word Search

Find your favorite characters
from Ariel's Undersea Adventure
in the word search.

```
C I R E D V Q E R C O O H B L
A C O N G E I F L Z O I D B J
I D H D S C L E H O N Q X G Y
E I A Q J O H L D U M H C C I
S J C C U I S T S V W J D Q H
V X U N K A U T G O C B O L A
H F D I L V L U A M D Q J R N
E E J U B Z M C L A Y L I E O
R I S G E Q C S Z S T E S T R
A R J E T S A M G T L M A U P
U P G Q X L T F Y O C M X N V
E M Y H B L S K R L B S F D D
N A I T S A B E S F G F K W V
Q Z S Q H W X W L M A P A J S
T D P W N R Q U N J T C A Y C
```

Ariel	Jetsam
Eric	Scuttle
Flotsam	Sebastian
Flounder	Ursula

Check the answer key on page 158
to see the completed word search.

If you're hungry, the place to visit is **Pacific Wharf**. Here you'll find great restaurants and the Ghirardelli chocolate factory. Don't miss the **Boudin Bakery** tour. You'll learn about the mother dough that is the basis for San Francisco's famous **sourdough bread**. It is more than 150 years old.

World of Color is a spectacular **nighttime water show** that cost $75 million to design and build. It has more than **1,000** fountains that can shoot water up to **200** feet high. There is also a **380-foot** mist screen that images can be projected upon. Look out for the firewhips. They shoot flames up to **50** feet into the air!

Opened in 2004, **The Twilight Zone Tower of Terror** features a haunted elevator that **plunges guests** down an elevator shaft. For two very long minutes, guests fall again and again, including one **drop of 13 stories**. It is the tallest ride in California Adventure and the tallest building in Anaheim, California.

If you like the movie *Monsters, Inc.*, visit **Mike & Sulley to the Rescue!** On this wild taxicab ride, you'll visit **Harryhausen's sushi restaurant**. Menu items include Terrible Teriyucki and Assorted Yukitori. The restaurant was named after the famous animator Ray Harryhausen.

Radiator Springs Racers cost $200 million to build. It's one of the most expensive rides ever created. And what do you get for $200 million? A two-car all-out race at 40 miles per hour through the 12-acre world of the *Cars* movies.

ANSWER KEY

PAGE 47

```
W H L Q E O A J L J Y Z V A Z
K I F L G M J O F W H S K P P
I W J D T A B W J X Q S E U H
B L E A R I E L P Y S X R E G
X L E L L E B P F U R E H F V
R A U Y Z K X A V V W U M J V
F B H E A V A I U O T F N O C
H O O C V I Y Z L R A X Z M G
Y V M I E W H F N U O R L L R
E O Y L S F S K N E C R O W O
P N M A L J S A S U O Z A O K
O Q I O U I E W D N J I X Y B
U C R L W D F G O S S C Z R I
B A Z K A M E M T Y E F M H B
L O Y M B F C G W Z H H L P Q
```

PAGE 124

```
F Y K A G Z J H J B X M Q X K
O P G D E U S R E H Y Z M W A
Z O A B E Y O M F K Y J M Z N
H O I W I T T P G Z I I A R G
E H J Q D Z Q U B A I S O A A
E L B W Q D S M Y S Q C I B J
Q N D R P I Y Z A I H E S B M
I V R C F H I T E L G I P I F
X E E Y O R E I A D L L V T P
O B U R E G G I T W N K W S A
K Q Z K U A S A O Y Q Q Z V W
Q M F M Y G F Y D D M P A F C
F Z Z A Z M S U J S D H P U O
C G Z Y Q Z A I Z Q F Q S P C
Q Z L A Z Z O K U Q K O O R S
```

PAGE 78

```
H E O C P V F R N N H W X H L
H K U F N E E D K A I X V A S
I F F I E R Q I E U M N J E E
V S L P O X V Q R T U E M J R
Q G E L L B X E N I S C O U T
N V P Q D L R Z X L R D D Y L
N X E K M A F W H U A M X Z V
E P Y S F H T L E S F H Y B P
S N C A J V U R A H B H J J
Q C E I R O Q E A Z M X Z A O
O S Q I Y W N F F N H D G T U
M Y Y A W I R K M K O R K T M
L Q G P R H W B T D A G V U Y
U E Y A N E P T U N E F R O P
R W M Z Z H J Z V P Y A L A N
```

PAGE 152

```
C I R E D V Q E R C O O H B L
A C O N G E I F L Z O I D B J
I D H D S C L E H O N Q X G Y
E I A Q J O H L D U M H C C I
S J C C U I S T S V W J D Q H
V X U N K A U T G O C B O L A
H F D I L V L U A M D Q J R N
E E J U B Z M C L A Y L I E O
R I S G E Q C S Z S T E S T R
A R J E T S A M G T L M A U P
U P G Q X L T F Y O C M X N V
E M Y H B L S K R L B S F D D
N A I T S A B E S F G F K W V
Q Z S Q H W X W L M A P A J S
T D P W N R Q U N J T C A Y C
```

We hope you've enjoyed this brief tour through the secrets and highlights of Disneyland. While we've packed the book with information, there is so much more for you to discover. So start exploring and compiling secrets of your own!

If you enjoyed *Secrets of Disneyland*, check out *Secrets of Walt Disney World*! It has lots of **little-known facts** about Walt Disney World, the largest of all the Disney parks.